D0768785

I Know Someone with Down Syndrome

Vic Parker

Heinemann Library
Chicago, Illinois

www.heinemannraintree.com
Visit our website to find out more information about Heinemann-Raintree books.

To order:

☎ Phone 888-454-2279

💻 Visit www.heinemannraintree.com to browse our catalog and order online.

Edited by Rebecca Rissman, Daniel Nunn, and Siân Smith
Designed by Joanna Hinton Malivoire
Picture research by Mica Brancic
Originated by Capstone Global Library
Printed in the United States of America by Worzalla Publishing

14 13 12 11 10
10 9 8 7 6 5 4 3 2 1

Library of Congress Cataloging-in-Publication Data
Parker, Victoria.
  I know someone with down syndrome / Vic Parker.
     p. cm. — (Understanding health issues)
  Includes bibliographical references and index.
  ISBN 978-1-4329-4558-9 (hc)
  ISBN 978-1-4329-4574-9 (pb)
  1. Down Syndrome—Juvenile literature. I. Title.
  RC571.P39 2011
  616.85'8842—dc22   2010026419

Acknowledgments
We would like to thank the following for permission to reproduce photographs: Alamy p. 15 (© Steve Skjold); Corbis pp. 12 (Design Pics/© Leah Warkentin), 21, 22 (© Mika), 25 (© Gabe Palmer); Getty Images pp. 5 (Aurora/Rhea Anna), 9 (Stockbyte/George Doyle), 18 (Realistic Reflections), 23 (Designs pics); Karen Gaffney p. 27; © Newspix p. 15 (News Ltd/Peter Clark); PA p. 14 (John Birdsall/John Birdsall); Photolibrary pp. 4 (Design Pics Inc/Kristy-Anne Glubish), 8 (Moodboard), 10 (Corbis), 11 (Peter Arnold Images/Ed Reschke); Press Association pp. 17 (EMPICS Sport/Nigel French), 20 (The Washington Time/Landov); Science Photo Library pp. 6, 7 (JOTI), 13 (James King-Holmes); The Kobal Collection p. 26 (Warner Bros TV).

Cover photograph of a girl with Down Syndrome relaxing on snow after skiing reproduced with permission of iStockphoto.com (© Diloute).

We would like to thank Matthew Siegel, Ashley Wolinski, and Stuart Mills for their invaluable help in the preparation of this book.

Every effort has been made to contact copyright holders of any material reproduced in this book. Any omissions will be rectified in subsequent printings if notice is given to the publisher.

Contents

Some words are printed in bold, **like this**. You can
find out what they mean in the glossary.

Do You Know Someone with Down Syndrome?

You might have a friend with Down Syndrome. Down Syndrome is a **medical condition** that people are born with. It affects people's bodies and their learning abilities, too.

Someone you know could have Down Syndrome.

People with Down Syndrome enjoy the same things as everyone else.

Down Syndrome is not a disease, and people who have it do not usually feel sick. They can live active, happy lives.

How Does Down Syndrome Affect People?

People with Down Syndrome are all different. It can take young children with Down Syndrome longer to learn some skills. These might include walking, talking, doing difficult tasks with their hands, reading, and remembering things.

Children with Down Syndrome may seem younger than other children who are the same age.

Some people with Down Syndrome use **sign language** or pictures to help them explain what they mean.

If the effects of Down Syndrome are very strong, then some people may not be able to learn some skills fully. They may need more help and to find other ways to do things.

Some people with mild Down Syndrome are very good at different hobbies.

Other people are only mildly affected by Down Syndrome. They may learn to do certain skills, such as painting pictures, better than other people without Down Syndrome.

This man with Down Syndrome works in a busy office.

Many people with Down Syndrome go on to do exactly the same things that other people do. They can go to school and college, have jobs, and get married.

The Cause of Down Syndrome

Our bodies are made up of millions of pieces too small to see, called **cells**. Every cell contains a tiny thread of information. This tells our bodies how to grow and **develop**.

You can see cells if you use a piece of equipment called a **microscope**.

People with Down Syndrome have extra bits of this thread of information in their cells. This tells their bodies to grow and develop differently in some ways than the bodies of other people.

This is what a human body cell looks like through a microscope.

Who Gets Down Syndrome?

Babies born with Down Syndrome can be smaller than other babies.

Any baby can have Down Syndrome, no matter what the race or nationality of their parents. Older mothers are more likely to have babies with Down Syndrome than younger mothers.

About 1 in every 800 to 1,000 babies born has Down Syndrome. If someone is born with Down Syndrome, it will never go away. If you are not born with it, you cannot get it later.

Many scientists are working to find out why some people are born with Down Syndrome.

At School

Some children with Down Syndrome go to special schools, where they can have expert help with learning. Everybody has different ways that they learn best.

Children at special schools have more one-on-one attention from teachers than at an ordinary school.

Holding and using a pen can be difficult for some people with Down Syndrome.

Many children with Down Syndrome go to ordinary schools. Some have assistants to help them. They may also have special classes for learning things they find harder.

At Play

We can all learn new things through playing.

All children love to play. Some games and activities can help children with Down Syndrome improve their **coordination** or movement skills.

Children with Down Syndrome often enjoy exercise, such as dancing or sports. Some take part with children without Down Syndrome, while others take part in competitions or teams especially for people with **disabilities**.

These soccer players with Down Syndrome are playing in a tournament.

Spending Time with Others

Having good friends makes life fun.

Children with Down Syndrome have the same feelings as everyone else. If they are left out, they will feel hurt and sad. So, treat them the same as your other friends.

Children with Down Syndrome like joining in with everybody. We are all happier when we have friends around. People with Down Syndrome can be very caring, loyal friends.

Friends can share many great times together.

Health Problems

People with Down Syndrome can catch colds and coughs more often than someone else. They may also have problems with their sight, hearing, or how food passes through their bodies.

This girl with Down Syndrome wears a **hearing aid** to help with her hearing.

Many people with Down Syndrome wear glasses to help with their sight.

However, all these things can be helped with medical care, so they can live healthy lives. Some people with Down Syndrome do not have any health problems at all.

Growing Older with Down Syndrome

People with Down Syndrome can grow up to make choices for themselves. They may choose to live in places where there are people to help them. They may be able to live on their own or with a partner, and they may have jobs.

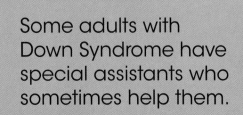

Some adults with Down Syndrome have special assistants who sometimes help them.

People with Down Syndrome can live into their sixties or even longer.

People with Down Syndrome get older just like everyone else. Sometimes people get confused more easily or begin to forget things as they get old. This can happen earlier to people with Down Syndrome.

Being a Good Friend

There are many ways you can be a good friend to someone with Down Syndrome. Some of these are shown in the list below.

You can:

- play games that you both enjoy
- help your friend with difficult tasks, but do not take over or do everything for him or her
- stick up for each other if you need to.

We all have different bodies and personalities.

Living with Down Syndrome can be difficult at times. We are all different in many ways. A good friend likes us and values us for who we are.

Famous People with Down Syndrome

American Luke Zimmerman has always loved acting. He once played the lead role in Shakespeare's play *Romeo and Juliet*. He is a student at a performing arts college and appears on television regularly.

Luke Zimmerman stars in a television show called *The Secret Life of the American Teenager*.

Karen Gaffney enjoys all sorts of different swimming challenges.

Karen Gaffney is such a good swimmer that she swam in a six-person team across a sea, all the way from England to France. She has also studied at college to be a teaching assistant.

Down Syndrome: Facts and Fiction

Facts

- Down Syndrome is named after Dr. John Langdon Down, who was the first person to recognize the **medical condition**, in 1866.

- About 3,357 babies are born with Down Syndrome in the United States each year.

Fiction

(?) People with Down Syndrome are always happy.

> **WRONG!** They have the same wide range of feelings and moods as everyone else.

(?) People with Down Syndrome all look the same.

> **WRONG!** There are some physical features that some people with Down Syndrome can share. But people with Down Syndrome will always look more like the members of their family than they look like other people with Down Syndrome.

Glossary

cells smallest unit that makes up living things

coordination ability to move in a skilled, balanced way

develop to change as something grows older

disability illness, injury, or condition that makes it difficult for someone to do the things that other people do

hearing aid special device that helps a person to hear

medical condition health problem that a person has for a long time or for life

microscope device that makes very small objects look larger, so people can study them

sign language way of communicating using hands and fingers

Find Out More

Books to Read

Bryan, Jenny. *I Have Down Syndrome* (*Taking Care of Myself*). New York: Gareth Stevens, 2011.

Doering Tourville, Amanda. *My Friend Has Down Syndrome* (*Friends with Disabilities*). Mankato, Minn.: Picture Window, 2010.

Powell, Jillian. *Luke Has Down's Syndrome* (*Like Me, Like You*). Langhorne, Pa.: Chelsea Clubhouse, 2005.

Websites

http://kidshealth.org/parent/medical/genetic/down_syndrome.html
Visit Kids' Health to learn more about Down Syndrome.

www.ndss.org
Find out lots of information about Down Syndrome at this National Down Syndrome Society website.

Index